D1516513

The words of the wise and their dark sayings
(*Book of Proverbs*)

The proverb cannot be bettered
(*Irish Proverb*)

When a fool is told a proverb,
its meaning has to be explained
(*Ashanti Proverb*)

Proverbs & Sayings of Ireland

Edited by
Séan Gaffney & Seamus Cashman

MJF Books
New York

Published by MJF Books
Fine Communications
322 Eighth Avenue
New York, NY 10001

Proverbs and Sayings of Ireland
LC Control Number 2005935800
ISBN-13: 978-1-56731-759-6
ISBN-10: 1-56731-759-6

CONTENTS

ACKNOWLEDGEMENTS

It is with particular pleasure that we welcome this latest
edition of the ever popular *Proverbs and Sayings of
Ireland*, and we are pleased to take this opportunity to
thank the many thousands of readers who have purchased
and, we trust, enjoyed this book down the years. We also
acknowledge and thank Billy Merwick who provided the
decorative illustrations which enhanced all the previous
editions of the book, and we congratulate him and wish
him all the best in the future. The Robert Gibbings
woodcuts chosen for this new edition wonderfully reflect
the traditional and rural ethos of the proverbs themselves.

ACKNOWLEDGEMENTS FROM THE FIRST EDITION

We acknowledge with gratitiude the contributions and
encouragement of many friends, in particular our parents,
Ann and James Cashman, and Margaret Gaffney. A special
word of thanks to Margaret Ryan, Deirdre Duffy, Monica
Miller, Joy Adams, John Logue and Paul Walsh.

INTRODUCTION

The proverb cannot be bettered – Though the proverb is abandoned, it cannot be falsified – how true these are readers will best discover for themselves in the following collection of Irish proverbs, sayings and triads. The triad is perhaps the most fascinating type of saying and though little used today in the non-Irish speaking parts of the country, it is still to be heard in the Gaeltacht areas, in West Cork, Galway and the Aran Islands.

A glance through the index of key words reveals the range of the Irish proverb, its themes, and the imagery and symbols used. As might be expected, the reputed vulnerability of our race to religion and romanticism is well represented. But the story the proverb tells is not quite that of a priest-ridden peasantry content in their poverty. Rather it shows us to have – or at least to have had – a subtle, sly perhaps, but generally humorous self-confidence. 'The priest's pig' may get 'the most porridge'; but the proverb also advises us to be 'neither intimate nor distant with the clergy'! Nor are we shown to be wholly susceptible to romanticism: 'it's better to be lucky than to be an early riser' but 'there's no success without authority and laws'. The proverbs reveal a deep conviction in a relationship between the spiritual and the material that is both challenging and realistic.

Proverbs are, in a sense, a race's unconscious expression of its moral attitudes. Our proverbs seem frequently to take the form of a national confession of sins: the evils of drink, gambling, greed, vanity, improvidence abound. But the virtues are there: faith, gentleness, love of nature, tolerance, and a trust in a life after death that offers a constant check to the materialism already mentioned.

Irish proverbs are rich in nature symbolism and imagery: the wind, the sea, the mountains; plants, animals, birds and fishes. The kingfisher, mackerel, thistle, plover, the horse and the hare, even the common crow are all called upon to mirror our achievements, hopes and failings.

While the proverbs of a race are often readily identifiable as belonging to that race, the ideas expressed and the images used touch on matters more fundamental than a national identity. One can readily accept that Irish proverbs should have their exact counterparts among the proverbs of other Celtic races. There are numerous examples of similarities among the sayings of the Irish, Welsh and Scottish – A long illness doesn't lie (Irish); To be long sick and to die nevertheless (Welsh); Marriage at the dungheap and the Godparents far away (Irish); Marriage o'er the anvil, sponsorship o'er the sea (Scottish); A drink is shorter than a story (Irish and Manx); Bribery splits a stone (Scottish). Such typical proverbs as these listed here also have their counterparts in most European languages.

However, it is interesting to discover that our proverbs also have affinities with those of races as far distant as the West Indies and Africa. Among Jamaican people, who are of African descent, there is a saying: 'When you sleep wid darg, you ketch him flea'. Our equivalent is : 'He who lies with dog rises with fleas'. We speak of sending the goose on a message to the foxes' den; the Hausa of West Africa have: 'Even if the hyena's town is destroyed , one does not send a dog in to trade'.

Irish proverbs and sayings derive from two mainstreams: the gaelic tradition, in the Irish language, and the anglo-Irish tradition, in the English language. Both reflect the strong biblical influence found in the proverbs throughout 'western' countries. This collection includes some of the oldest seanfhocail (old sayings) recorded in Ireland as well as sayings of more recent origin. But it is by no means exhaustive. The exact origins of most of these sayings are unknown: perhaps a throw-away phrase; perhaps a line of a poem long forgotten – who knows? It is what survives that matters.

For readers interested in pursuing the Irish Proverb further, a brief word on some sources. Several substantial collections have been published (from which many in this collection have been taken, and which we gratefully acknowledge.) Most of these are unfortunately long out of print. The most recent, and certainly the finest is T. S. O'Maille, ed., *Sean-fhocala Chonnacht*, 2 vols. (Dublin, 1948-52). Others are: T.O'Donoghue, ed., *Sean-fhocail na Mumhain*, a Gaelic League publication, 1902; E. Ua Muirgheasa, ed., *Sean fhocla Uladh*, (1907) which contains English translations as does T.F. O'Rahilly, *A Miscellany of Irish Proverbs*, (Dublin 1922). Shorter collections will be found in J. O'Daly, *Irish Language Miscellany*, Burke, *Irish Grammar*; Hardiman, *Irish Minstrelsy*, 2 vols reissued by IUP in 1969; the *Gaelic Journal* and *The Ulster Journal of Archaeology*. P. W. Joyce , *English as we speak it in Ireland*, (Dublin 1910) is a useful and entertaining starting point though of limited use for proverbs. Two important sources still to be fully researched are the Douglas Hyde 'Diaries' in the National Library of Ireland, and the manuscript collections of the Irish Folklore Department in UCD, in particular the 'Schools Mss.' for anglo-Irish proverbs. *Bealoideas* the journal of the Folklore Commission includes lists of proverbs in its various issues. Information on further sources will be found in bibliographies in the published works mentioned.

Most of the proverbs in this collection have been translated from the Irish language. English translations of proverbs in the Irish language are not always successful. We have endeavoured to remain as close to the original as possible. An illustration of the effects of translation, however, can be readily seen by comparing 'One beetle recognises another' with the original Irish proverb 'Aithníonn ciaróg ciaróg eile'. The impact of the expression depends greatly on the sound of the word ciaróg, and its repetition. The pattern cannot be reproduced satisfactorily in English; and the word 'beetle' is by comparison with the Irish word, weak and ineffectual.

We have classified each proverb by subject recognising that such classification is both limiting and subjective. For proverbs are by their very nature elusive and usually defy adequate classification under any one heading. However as the index contains the key-words of each proverb, our arrangement should cause the reader little difficulty.

Classifications

The proverbs are listed in this book alphabetically under the following headings. The Index of Key Words at the end of the book will guide the reader to specific proverbs.

Ability	Conversation	Fair-haired
Advice	Courtship	Fame
Affectation	Criticism	Familiarity
Age	Cunning	Fate
Anger	Curses	Fear
Appearance	Cynicism	Fighting
Art	Danger	Flattery
As....as...	Death	Flimsiness
Beauty	Debt	Food
Betrayer	Deception	Fool
Bitterness	Delusion	Foolishness
Blessings	Desire	Forgiveness
Boastings	Despair	Fortune
Borrowing	Devil	Frail
Bravery	Discipline	Freedom
Bribery	Dismissal	Friendship
Carelessness	Drink	Futility
Caution	Economy	Gambling
Change	Education	Generosity
Character	Effort	Gentleness
Charity	Egotism	God
Chastity	Eloquence	Goodness
Children	Endurance	Gossip
Choice	English, The	Gratitude
Clergy	Equality	Greed
Coincidence	Error	Grief
Comfort	Evil	Happiness
Compromise	Excused	Health
Contentment	Experience	Home

Honesty
Honour
Hope
Humility
Humour
Hunger
Idleness
Ignorance
Impossibility
Independence
Inequality
Initiative
Intelligence
Involvement
Irishman
Judgement
Justice
Kerry
Kindness
Kinship
Knowledge
Law
Laziness
Leadership
Lies
Life
Love
Luck
Manners
Marriage
Maturity
Meanness
Men
Misfortune

Mother
Nature
Neatness
Necessity
Nobility
Obedience
Obligation
Ownership
Participation
Patience
Patriotism
Peace
Perception
Pity
Poetry
Possession
Poverty
Power
Presumption
Pride
Procrastination
Promise
Proverbs
Prudence
Red-hair
Repentance
Reputation
Revenge
Rogue
Rumour
Scarcity
Seasons
Secret
Self-destruction

Selfishness
Sense
Separation
Shame
Shyness
Silence
Strength
Stupidity
Success
Suitability
Tact
Talent
Talkativeness
Thrift
Time
Treachery
Trouble
Trust
Truth
Understanding
Uselessness
Value
Vanity
Warning
Wastefulness
Wealth
Weather
Welcome
Widow
Wisdom
Woman
Work
Youth

Ability	No one can tell what he is able to do till he tries	1
	You can't whistle and chew meal at the same time	2
	You can't bark and run at the same time	3
	A vessel only holds its fill	4
	Often the hound that was made fun of killed the deer	5
	The strong man may when he wants to; the weak man when he's able	6
	The gobadán (kingfisher) cannot work both tides	7
Advice	Don't give cherries to pigs; don't give advice to a fool	8
	A man is often a bad adviser to himself and a good adviser to another	9
	The man who won't have advice will have conflict	10
	He is bad that will not take advice, but he is a thousand times worse that takes every advice	11
	The cat is his own best adviser	11a
	Crafty advice is often got from a fool	12
	A wise man takes advice	13
Affectation	A ring on her finger and not a stitch of clothes on her back	14

Sparing at home and lavish in the hospital 15

Like the sun on the hill-top, but like a thistle
on the hearth 16

Street angel, house devil 17

Age When the twig hardens, it's difficult to twist it 18

A man lives long in his native place 19

It's hard to teach an old dog to dance 20

As the cock crows, the young bird chirrups 21

To be old and decayed dishonours no-one 22

In youth we have our troubles before us;
in age we leave pleasure behind 23

Young people don't know what age is;
old people forget what youth was 24

The old man hasn't the place of the cat in the ashes 25

Is it not a lonesome thing to be getting old 26

Anger There's anger in an open laugh 27

Old burdens don't incite blows 28

Red-hot ashes are easily rekindled 29

No wrong to be done to seven classes of persons
excited to anger:— a bard, a chief, a woman,
a prisoner, a drunken person, a druid,
and a king in his own dominions   30

Appearance   An inch is a great deal in a man's nose   31

It's not the bones that are beautiful
but the flesh on the shoulders   32

A thong is no shorter for having been in water   33

Its appearances are better than its value   34

Handsome is as handsome does   35

A black hen lays white eggs   36

A buckle is a great addition to an old shoe   37

Art   Nobility listens to art   38

As ... as   As stiff as a poker   39

As tough as a wheelstring   40

As mim as a dog without his tail   41

As black as Toal's cloak   42

As bad as Barringtons's blood hound to us   43

A localised Kerry expression. When the Irishwere being hunted down in Penal
timesa particularly vicious duo, a Captain Barringtonand Colonel Nelson used
a bloodhound to chasetheir quarry which savaged the victim terribly,hence
giving rise to the saying.

As old as Atty Hayes' goat   44

A Cork expression. The story goes that the goat belonged to Atwell Hayes
who was father of Sir Henry Hayes, sherrif of Cork in 1790. The goat was
reputed to be old even when Atty was a young man. A generation later
Captain Philip Allen, son-in-law of Sir Henry Hayes became mayor of Cork,

(in 1800) and gave a civil banquet to celebrate the occasion. At this time the goat died and Allen being a bit of a joker served up the hind quarters of the goat unknowingly to his guests, as venison. The 'venison' was proclaimed by the city fathers as delicious. In county Armagh the corresponding expression is 'As old as Killylea bog'.

As wise as the women of Mungret   45

A Limerick expression. The amusing story attached to this saying concerns the monastic foundation and school at Mungret. A number of scholars was sent from Cashel to compete with their Mungret counterparts. However the Limerick scholars fearing defeat and the loss of their reputation dressed as washerwomen and waited along the roadside, washing in the nearby river. As the Cashel contingent approached and asked the 'women' for directions they were completely taken aback when answered in perfect Greek. Thinking that if the washerwomen were so learned then the scholars must be unusually brilliant, the poor Tipperary monks turned for home, leaving the reputation of Mungret intact and untarnished!

As hard as the hob of hell	46
As cunning as the fox	47
As long as a wet Sunday	48
As old as the hills	49

16

As ... as

As melodious as a lark 70

As brave as Fionn MacCumhall (*see notes*) 71

As yellow as a ragweed *(ragworth)* 72

As lazy as a donkey 73

As lazy as a piper's luidin *(little finger)* 73a

As busy as a bee 74

As salty as the sea 75

As good as gold 76

As rich as Damer 77

A Dublin expression, not in common usage. The story is based on Joseph Damer, born in 1630. After serving Cromwell he returned to Ireland where he purchased much land forfeited in the Williamite confiscations. He became a banker and achieved much noteriety as a miser. He died in 1720 leaving nearly half a million pounds, a phenomenal amount even by to-day's standards. Johnathan Swift was moved, as was his wont, to comment unfavourably on Mr. Damer:

The ghost of old Damer who left not his betters
When it heard of a bank appear'd to his debtors
And lent them for money the backs of his letters
His debtors they wonder'd to find him so frank,
For old Nick gave the papers the mark of the bank.

	God bless three times, and three spits for luck (*said at the birth of a calf*)	95a
Boasting	There are two heads on all his sheep	96
Borrowing	The law of borrowing is to break the borrower	97
	The borrowed horse has hard hoofs	98
	The loan of something on loan	99
	Don't exchange your horse when you are crossing the river	100
	He who is bad to give the loan is good for directing you	101
Bravery	The brave man never loses	102
	Every dog is valiant at his own door	103
	Every hound is brave on his own dunghill	104
	Every man is bold until he faces a crowd	105
Bribery	Bribe the rogue and you need have no fear of the honest man	106
	Beware of the bribed man	107
	Bribery will split a stone	108
	Hold on to the bone and the dog will follow you	109
Carelessness	Loose and careless like the leg of a pot	110
	A ship is often lost because of one man	111
	By their tongues people are caught, and by their horns, cattle	112

Every mother thinks it is on her own child
the sun rises   164

An inch of a lad is better than a foot of a girl   165

No man ever wore a cravat as nice as
his own child's arm around his neck   166

Your son is your son to-day, but your daughter
is your daughter forever   167

Choice

If the bare part of the hill is bad,
the summit is worse   168

It can't be both curds and whey with you   169

It's difficult to choose between two blind goats   170

Clergy

The priest's pig gets the most porridge   171

Although there was nobody present but the priest
and the friar still I have lost all my property   172

A dumb priest never got a parish   173

If there is a hen or a goose it's surely on the
priest's table it will be   174

It is his own child the priest baptises first   175

Be neither intimate nor distant with the clergy   176

A priest that's made a pet of and a pig that's
made a pet of are the two worst pets of all   177

The way of the nuns with the country-women
– they receive a great lump and give a small return   178

Give the priest his own side of the road   179

Don't be the mean and don't be generous
with the clergy   180

Cunning	He would cover a rock with hay and sell it for a haycock	195
	He would skin a louse and send the hide and fat to market	196
	He would build a nest in your ear	197

In spite of the fox's cunning, his skin is often sold	198
He'd steal the cross of an ass's back	199
He would steal the egg from the crane and finally the crane herself	200
Cunning is better than strength	201

Curses	The curse does not fall on a stick or a stone	202
	A bad death to you	203
	Bad cess to you (*see notes*)	203a
	A heart-burning on you	204
	A cold day on you	205
	The raven's curse on you	206
	The kittens death to you	207
	May your trouble be in your throat	208

	The curse of Cromwell on you	208a
Cynicism	It's a very good time if it lasts	209
	When the sky falls we'll all catch larks	210
Danger	The man who loves danger shall perish in it	211
	No staying in dangerous roads	212
	A lion is not a safe companion for all persons	213
	A horse on a cliff or a cow in a swamp, two in danger	213a
Death	Many a day we shall rest in the clay	214
	Death is the poor man's best physician	215
	Death doesn't come without a cause	216
	There's neither herb nor cure for death	217
	To die and to lose one's life are much the same thing	218
	There'll be many a dry eye at his death	219
	There is hope from the mouth of the sea but none from the mouth of the grave	220
	A man at sea may return but not the man in the churchyard	221
	Sleep is the brother (or the image) of death	222

One can't tell which skin will hang from
the rafter first, the old sheep's or the lamb's   223

The trace of the hand will live but
not the hand that made it   224

Death stares the old in the face and lurks behind the
backs of the young   225

Nimble as the hare is she is caught at last   226

There is many a person with a high head to-day
who will be lying lowly tomorrow   227

May God spare anyone who has a hand in his
own death   228

You will never comb a grey head   229

It is not the tree that is a long time shaking
that is the first to fall   230

Death does not take a bribe   231

The graveyard growth is in him   232

Death never comes too late   233

You'll be going yet and your two feet before you   234

	An old cat will not burn himself	315
	Sense bought (i.e. experience) is better than two senses learned	316
	You can't put an old head on young shoulders	317
	Every hound is a pup till he hunts	317a
Fair-haired	If I am yellow I have a fair heart	318
Fame	Fame lasts longer than life	319
	Without money fame is dead	320
	Falling is easier than rising	321
	Greatness knows modesty	322
Familiarity	To know somebody, (one must) live in the same house with him	323
	Too much of one thing is the same as nothing	324
	Familiarity breeds contempt	325
	People of the same trade are friendly	326
Fate	Long as the day may be night comes at last	327
	He that is born to be hanged needn't fear water	328
	Every nursling as it is nursed, every web as it is woven	329
	Pity the man drowned in the storm; for after the rain comes the sunshine	330
	The darkest hour is nearest dawn	331
	A ship is often lost by the harbour	332

	No matter how often a pitcher goes to the water, it is broken in the end	333
	No matter how long the day, night comes	334
	What kills one man gives life to another	335
	About the foot of the tree the foliage falls	336
Fear	Fear is a fine spur, so is rage	337
	Be afraid, and you'll not meet danger	338
	The man who is struck on the head, will afterwards be afraid	339
Fighting	To fight like Kilkenny cats	340

In 1798 when the Hessians were quartered in Kilkenny they amused themselves by tying two cats tails together and throwing them over a line, to fight. Their officer on hearing of this, ordered his men to stop. However the soldiers continued the practice in secret, and one day while they were amusing themselves in this manner they heard the officer approaching. One soldier drawing his sword cut down the cats leaving only their tails hanging. When the officer enquired as to where the cats were, the soldier replied that the cats had fought so furiously that they had devoured all but each other's tails. The story proved immensely popular - but it is probably just a tall tale!

	Quarrelsome dogs get dirty coats	341
	Don't kick till you're spurred	342
	Be warning but not striking	343
	A word goes to the wind but a blow goes to the bones	344
	Wine is better than blood	345
	There is often the death of a person between two words	346

You can take the horse to the well,
but you can't make him drink — 384

Friendship
No war is as bitter as a war between friends,
but it doesn't last long — 385

Reverence ceases once blood is spilled — 386

Two persons never lit a fire without disagreeing — 387

If you will walk with lame men
you will soon limp yourself — 388

There was never a scabby sheep in a flock
that didn't like to have a comrade — 389

The man long absent is forgotten — 390

In times of trouble friends are recognised — 391

A friend's eye is a good mirror — 392

Reckoning up is the ending of friendship — 393

The friend that can be bought is not worth buying — 394

If I like the sow
I like her litter — 395

Prove your friend
before you need
him — 396

A little
relationship is
better than much
friendship — 397

Futility

It's hard to fight with the wide ocean   425

An empty bag won't stand   426

'Tis hard to drive a hare out of a bush he's not in   427

You can't draw blood out of a turnip   428

You won't make a rope from the sand of the sea   429

It's only the Lord can make a racehorse
out of a jackass   430

The devil couldn't do it unless he was drunk   431

'Tis no use talking when the harm is done   432

Gambling

It is the
hope of
recompense
that ruins
the
card-player   433

Better a son
a gambler
than a
drinker   434

The expectation of success is what
beggars the gambler   435

Generosity A big belly was never generous   436

A generous man, they say, has never gone to hell   437

Wide is the door of the little cottage   438

As you have burned the candle, give the inch   439

	Take gifts with a sigh, most men give to be paid	440
	O'Neill's gift and his two eyes looking after it (*see notes*)	441
	It is worth going to meet generosity that is slow	442
Gentleness	A gentle answer quenches anger	443
	A kind word never broke anyone's mouth	444
God	God's help is nearer than the door	445
	God is not as severe as he is said to be	446
	God often pays debts without money	447
	God moves slowly yet his grace comes	448
	God never closes one door but he opens another	449
	God shares the good things	450
	The person not taught by God is not taught by man	451
	The love of God guides every good	452

A woman told me that a woman told her that
she saw a woman who saw a woman who made
ale of potatoes   467

The death of the old woman and the
marriage of the young woman   468

Talk by the fire is the talk of idle women   469

Gratitude   Sit on your heel and thank goodness for a new stool 470

You can't examine the teeth of a gift horse   471

Eaten bread is soon forgotten   472

I think little of buttermilk when I'm full of it   473

Strike a dog with a bone and he'll not growl   474

Thank God the right side of the house is out   475

Greed   One cannot take out of a sack
more than the full of it   476

If the cat had a churn her paw would often be in it   477

Though honey is sweet, do not lick it off a briar   478

The covetous man is always in want   479

He's not covetous but he'd fain have all   480

Don't refuse to sell your horse for the sake of a
crown   481

Eating and complaining like the greedy hen   482

A rag on every bush   483

Too many irons in the fire   484

A long illnesss doesn't lie   502

Beginning with a cough and ending with a coffin   503

A graveyard cough   504

The person who doesn't scatter the morning dew
will not comb grey hairs   505

One must pay health its tithes   506

The physician's hope, every misfortune   507

Patience is the cure for an old illness   508

Home   There is no fireside like your own fireside   509

It's a long way from home that the plover cries   509a

Honesty   When rogues disagree, honest men get their own   510

The man that steals stacks thinks
all the world thieves   511

Judgement	Don't make little of your dish for it may be an ignorant fellow who judges it	566
	Disputation in the heel of judgement	567
Justice	No merriment in the seat of justice	568
	Innocent or guilty, he'll be hanged said the judge	569
	There is little between justice and injustice	570
	Put justice before generosity	571
	Those who make laws should not break laws	572
	What is got badly goes badly	573
Kerry	Kerry security: bond, pledge, oath, and keep the money	574
Kindness	Pressure of the business weakens kindness	575
	The old hag is the better of being warmed, but the worse of being burned	576
Kinship	One beetle recognises another	577
	Blood is stronger than water	578
	One chafer knows another	579
	One thief knows another	580
	One pig knows another	581
	One liar knows another	582
	Great minds live apart, people may meet, but mountains and rocks never	583
Knowledge	A blind dog won't bark at the moon	584

Twenty years agrowing; twenty years at rest;
twenty years declining; and twenty years when
it doesn't matter whether you're there or not   616

Life is the true historian   617

Love Live in my heart and pay no rent   618

If you love the mother, you love her brood   619

They won't fall in love with the man they don't see   620

When the sight leaves the eye, love leaves the heart   621

After the settlement (the dowry), comes the love   622

Love is blind to blemishes and faults   623

Love hides ignominy and evil   624

Love is no impartial judge   625

House without hound, cat, or child,
house without love or affection   626

Love a woman or a child without their knowing it   627

To the raven her own chick is white   628

What is nearest the heart is usually nearest the lips   629

What is nearest the heart comes out   630

Love cools quickly   631

Love conceals ugliness, and hate sees a lot of faults   632

She who fills the heart, fills the eye   633

There's no love until there's a family   634

Absence makes the heart grow fond   635

Luck

It's better to be lucky than to be an early riser — 636

A chance shot will not kill the devil — 637

The man who has luck in the morning
has luck in the afternoon — 638

There's luck in sharing — 639

It's better to be lucky than wise — 640

A meeting in the sunlight is lucky,
and a burying in the rain — 641

The lucky person has only to be born — 642

Luck seldom lasts — 643

Manners

Without store no friends;
without rearing no manners — 644

Better good manners than good looks — 645

Marriage

The husband of the sloven is known in the field
amidst a crowd — 646

A growing moon and a flowing tide
are lucky times to marry in — 647

Never make a toil of pleasure, as the man said
when he dug his wife's grave only three feet deep — 648

Marriage at the dungheap and
the godparents
far away — 649

Woe to him
who does not
heed a good
wife's counsel — 650

Marriage

It's why women marry — the creatures,
God bless them, are too shy to say no   651

There was never an old slipper
but there was an old stocking to match it   652

A young man is bothered till he's married,
after that he's bothered entirely   653

There's only one thing in the world
better than a good wife.....no wife   654

The dowry falls over the cliff;
but the protruding lip remains on the wife   655

A bad wife takes advice from everyone
but her husband   656

He breaks his wife's head
and then buys a plaster for it   657

There are no trials till marriage   658

The carefree mother's daughter makes a bad wife   659

It's a lonesome washing that
there's not a (man's) shirt in   660

Marry a mountainy woman and you'll marry
the mountain   661

She's a good woman, but she didn't
take off her boots yet   662

The day you marry your wife
you marry your children   663

The blanket is the warmer of being doubled   664

She burnt her coal and did not warm herself   665

	He married money and got a woman with it	666
	Marry in haste and be sorry at your leisure	667
Maturity	By age or ability you're no child	668
Meanness	What you give wouldn't blind the eye of a midge	669
	As tight as tuppence in a market-woman's trashbag	670
	If you give the loan of your britches, don't cut off the buttons	671
	'Tis strange that the man who is so quick to find fault is himself so stingy about food	672
	To come with one hand longer than the other	673
	Nothing comes into a closed hand	674
Men	Some men are like bagpipes.... they can't speak till their bellies are filled	675
Misfortune	From the house of the devil to the house of the demon	676
	After misfortune the Irishman sees his profit	677
	It is well that misfortunes come one by one and not all together	678
	It's easy to sleep on the misfortune of others	679
	When misfortune is greatest relief is nearest	680
	There's worse than this in the North	681
	Nothing is ever as bad as it seems	682
	The old white horse is the end of all misfortune	683

	He got it from nature as the pig got the rooting in the ground	697
	Often a cow does not take after its breed	698
	What would a young cat do but eat mice?	699
	Nature will come through the claws, and the hound will follow the hare	700
	If you put a silk dress on a goat he is a goat still	701
	Every bird as it is reared and the lark for the bog	702
	What is in the marrow is hard to take out of the bone	703
	The wood will renew the foliage it sheds	704
	What will come from the briar but the berry	705
	The hand goes only where the leg goes	706
Neatness	A handstaff of holly, a buailtin of hazel, a single sheaf and a clean floor *(see notes)*	707
Necessity	One who is without cows must be his own dog	708
	Make necessity a virtue	709
	Necessity accepts no law	710
	A blind man can see his mouth	711
	You never miss the water till the well has run dry	712
Nobility	A king's son is not nobler than his food (see also number 38)	713
Obedience	Keep your tongue in your jaw and your toe in your pump	714

	Time and Patience would bring the snail to Jerusalem	728
Patriotism	Everyone praises his native land	729
Peace	Nobody ever bought peace but the man who hadn't got it	730
	Peace (quietness) is worth buying	731
	The world's quiet and the pig is in the sty	732
	Least said soonest mended	733
	No matter who succeeds or fails, the peacemaker will always suffer	734
	To the fighting man peace is sure	735
	The end of a feast is better than the beginning of a fight	736
Perception	An eye is blind in another man's corner	737
	One eye in the corner is sharper than two about the house	738
Pity	He's more to be pitied than laughed at	739
	Don't tell your complaint to one who has no pity	740
Poetry	A poem ought to be well made at first, for there is many a one to spoil it afterwards	741
Possession	It's better than it's want	742
	Have it yourself, or else do without it	743
	Better the certainty of the straddle (packsaddle) than the mere loan of a saddle	744

Possession is nine-tenths of the law	745
Better own a trifle than want a great deal	746
A wren in the hand is better than a crane to be caught	747
Possession satisfies	748
A bird in the hand is worth two in the bush	749
It's better than the loan you couldn't get	750
Half a loaf is better than no bread	751
A live dog is better than a dead lion	752
A trout in the pot is better than a salmon in the sea	753

Poverty

Put a beggar on horseback and he'll ride to hell	754
Put a beggar on horseback and he'll go on a gallop	755
Poverty parts good company	756
Poverty destroys companionship	757
Many a defect is seen in the poor man	758
It's hard to take britches off bare hips	759
The full man does not understand the wants of the hungry	760
A little pleases a poor man	761
Poor men take to the sea; the rich to the mountains	762
Poverty creates sadness	763
Pity the man who does wrong and is poor as well	764

There is nothing in the world so poor
as going to hell — 765

The thief is no danger to the beggar — 766

Poverty is no shame — 767

Two things that go to loss — turf on a mountain
and the wisdom of a poor man — 768

Shame is ever a part of poverty — 769

No-one is ever poor who has the sight of his eyes
and the use of his feet — 770

There is no tune without a penny — 771

A poor man never yet lost his property — 772

Poor is the church without music — 773

A smokey cabin, a handful of spuds and
a flea-filled bed — 774

Power No stopping the force of a going wheel by hand — 775

No forcing the sea — 776

Presumption Don't count your chickens before they are hatched — 777

Don't bless the fish till it gets to the land — 778

Don't build the sty until the litter comes — 779

	Praise the ripe field not the green corn	780
	Praise the ford when you have crossed it	781
	You must empty a box before you fill it again	782
Pride	The pride of women and the pride of priests	783
	It is difficult to soothe the proud	784
	Pride comes before a fall	785
	Pride feels no pain	786
	Pride is the author of every sin	787
	The jump of a cock on the dungheap	788
Procrastination	There is no virtue in the herb that is not got in time	789
	A postponement till morning a postponement for ever	790
	It is no time to go for the doctor when the patient is dead	791
Promise	A promise is a debt	792
Proverbs	Proverbs cannot be contradicted	793
	The proverb cannot be bettered	794
	Though the proverb is abandoned, it is not falsified	795
Prudence	Don't throw out the dirty water until you have the clean water in	796
	It's better to return from the centre of the ford than drown in the flood	797
	The sty before the litter	798

Red-hair	If you meet a red-haired woman, you'll meet a crowd	799
	To be red-haired is better than to be without a head	800
Repentance	To put off repentance is dangerous	801
	It's better to be sorry and stay than to be sorry and go away	802
Reputation	It's a small thing that outlives a man	803
	Remember even if you lose all, keep your good name for if you lose that you are worthless	804
	Those who get the name of rising early may lie all day	805
	When a man gets his feet in lime he cannot easily get rid of it	806
Revenge	No dealing with a revengeful man	807
Rogue	He was never good since the time a yard (of cloth) made a coat for him	808
	Don't mention him and a decent man in the one day	809
	A sly rogue is often in good dress	810
	She would drink the cream and say the cat she had was an old rogue	811
	The horse with the most scars is the one that highest kicks his rear	812
Rumour	The person who brings a story to you will take away two from you	813

A story without an author is not worth listening to 814

Leave the bad tale where you found it 815

There is no smoke without fire 816

(See also Gossip)

Scarcity	When all fruits fail welcome haws	817
	When the fruit is scarcest, its taste is sweetest	818
	We have a fine day more often than a kiln-cast	819
Seasons	A soft-dropping April brings milk to cows and sheep	820
	Autumn days come quickly like the running of a hound on the moor	821
	A misty winter brings a pleasant spring, a pleasant winter a misty spring	822
	Many a sudden change takes place on a spring day	823
	In winter the milk goes to the cow's horns	824
Secret	A secret is a weapon and a friend	825
	It is no secret that is known to three	826
	Fences (ditches) have ears	827

	Don't tell your secret even to a fence	828
	Woe to the man that entrusts his secrets to a ditch	829
	The secret of an old woman scolding	830
	If it's a secret, it's binding	831
	Don't tell secrets to the children of your relatives	832
Self-Destruction	No tree but has rotten wood enough to burn it	833
	A man may be his own ruin	834
	A wedge from itself splits the oak tree	835
	A man has often cut a rod to beat himself	836
Selfishness	It's for her own good that the cat purrs	837
	His own wound is what everyone feels soonest	838
	What is nearest the heart is nearest the mouth	839
	He who is best to me is he who shall get the best share	840
	The full stomach does not understand the empty one	841
	The man who was dividing Ireland didn't leave himself last	842
Sense	Sense doesn't come before age	843
Separation	After the gathering comes the scattering	844
Shame	What would shame him would turn back a funeral	845
	A fist full of gain and a village full of shame	846

	Better is the trouble that follows death	
	than the trouble that follows shame	847
Shyness	Do not keep your tongue under your belt	848
	A man is shy in another man's corner	849
Silence	A silent mouth is musical	850
	The silent are often guilty	851
	The silent mouth is sweet to hear	852
	When wrathful words arise a closed mouth	
	is soothing	853
	The stars make no noise	854
	Little talk is easy to cure	855
	A closed mouth — a wise head	856
	A silent mouth never did any harm	857
Strength	Strength is not enduring	858
Stupidity	Sending the goose on a message to the fox's den	859
	Putting the fox to mind the geese	860
	You didn't turn up when sense	
	was being distributed	861
Success	There's neither success nor efficiency	
	without authority and laws	862
	Fat is not to be had without labour	863
Suitability	The windy day is not the day for thatching	864
	One man's meat is another man's poison	865

| | Whoever the cap fits takes it | 866 |

Tact

| Better sit beside him than in his place | 867 |

| A short visit is best and that not too often | 868 |

| The eye should be blind in the home of another | 869 |

| It's often a man's mouth broke his nose | 870 |

| Don't say everything you want to say lest you hear something you would not like to hear | 871 |

| Don't let your tongue cut your throat | 872 |

| See not what you see and hear not what you hear | 873 |

| Never speak to the feet while the head is alive | 874 |

| Don't rest your eyes beyond what is your own | 875 |

| It's bad manners to talk about ropes in the house of a man whose father was hanged | 876 |

Talent

| A greyhound finds food in its feet | 877 |

| The slow hound often has good qualities | 878 |

| The bird that can sing and won't sing should be made to sing | 879 |

| A cat between two houses, a rabbit between two holes, the two liveliest | 879a |

Talkativeness   Great talk and little action   880

Treachery	He who spies is the one who kills	889
	Treachery returns	890
Trouble	There's trouble in every house and some in the street	891
	Everything troubles you and the cat breaks your heart	892
Trust	The fox never found a better messenger than himself	893
	Never trust a spiteful man	894
Truth	A man with a loud laugh makes truth itself seem folly	895
	Truth is great and will win out	896
	Even the truth may be bitter	897
	There are two tellings to every story	898
	Drunkenness and anger, 'tis said tell the truth	899
	What I'm afraid to hear I'd better say first myself	900
	Truth speaks even though the tongue were dead	901
	You can keep away from the rogue, but you cannot keep yourself safe from the liar	902
	Truth stands when everything else falls	903
	It is no shame to tell the truth	904
	Tell the truth and shame the devil	905
Understanding	The well-filled belly has little understanding of the empty	906

	'Tis afterwards that everything is understood	907
Uselessness	It's a bad hound that's not worth the whistling	908
	He knows how many grains to a bushel of wheat	909
	He knows the price of everything and the value of nothing	910
	He couldn't drag a herring off the coals	911
	It's just a wisp in place of a brush	912
Value	One pair of good soles is worth two pairs of upper leathers	913
	Without pressing too little or too hard, hold tight the reins for he's a fool who would not get value from a borrowed horse	914
	It's not worth a cuckoo-spit	915
	Better an idle house than a bad tenant	916
Vanity	Pity him who makes his opinion a certainty	917
	He thinks that he himself is the very stone that was hurled at the castle	918
	He dotes on his midden and thinks it the moon	919
Warning	That's a spoon ye'll sup sorrow with yet	920
Wastefulness	Wilful waste makes woeful want	921
Wealth	A shamefaced man seldom acquires wealth	922
	The money-maker (profiteer) is never tired	923
	The doorstep of a great house is slippery	924

	There is misfortune only where there is wealth	925
	Sweet is the voice of the man who has wealth	926
	A hut is a palace to a poor man	927
	A heavy purse makes a light heart	928
	There's little value in the single cow	929
	A man of one cow – a man of no cow	930
	It's easy to knead when meal is at hand	931
Weather	Wind from the east is good for neither man nor beast	932
	A Kerry shower is of twenty-four hours	933
	Better April showers than the breadth of the ocean in gold	934
Welcome	Better for a man to have even a dog welcome him than a dog bark at him	935
	Going in is not the same as going out	936
	A welcome is a debtor's face	937
Widow	What's all the world to a man when his wife is a widow	938
Wisdom	A wise head keeps a shut mouth	939
	Everyone is wise till he speaks	940
	Food is no more important than wisdom	941
	A contraction (in writing) is enough for a scholar	942
	The beginning of wisdom is the fear of God	943

There's no wise man without a fault   **944**

He may die of wind but he'll never die of wisdom   **945**

You can't put a wise head on young shoulders   **946**

Wisdom is what makes a poor man a king,
a weak person powerful,
a good generation of a bad one,
a foolish man reasonable   **947**

Though wisdom is good in the beginning,
it is better at the end   **948**

A little of anything isn't worth a pin; but a wee
bit of sense is worth a lot   **949**

No making of a wise man   **950**

Women

A dishonest woman can't be kept in and an honest
woman won't   **951**

There is no thing wickeder than a woman
of evil temper   **952**

A bad woman
(wife) drinks a lot of
her own bad
butter-milk   **953**

A foolish woman
knows a foolish
man's faults   **954**

A whistling woman
and a crowing hen
will bring no luck to
the house they are in   **955**

Women	Beef to the heels like a Mullingar heifer	956
	Eight lives for the men and nine for the women	957
	Wherever there are women there's talking, and wherever there's geese there's cackling	958
	Irishwomen have a dispensation from the Pope to wear the thick ends of their legs downwards	959
	Women are shy and shame prevents them from refusing a man	960
	Everything dear is a woman's fancy	961
	Like an Irish wolf she barks at her own shadow	962
	She wipes the plate with the cat's tail	963
	More hair than tit, like a mountain heifer	964
	Women are stronger than men, they do not die of wisdom	965
	When the old woman is hard pressed, she has to run	966
	It's difficult to trust a woman	967
	Man to the hills, woman to the shore	968
	Beat a woman with a hammer and you'll have gold	969
	'Tis as hard to see a woman cry, as a goose go barefoot	970
	'Where comes a cow,' the wise man lay down (St Colmcille), 'there follows a woman, and where comes a woman follows trouble'	971
	Only a fool would prefer food to a woman	972

Women

Don't be ever in court or a castle without a woman
to make your excuse   973

An excuse is nearer to a woman than her apron   974

There is nothing sharper than a woman's tongue   975

A woman without is she who has neither
pipe nor child   976

The yellow praiseach (kale) of the fields
that brings the Meath women to harm   977

A woman like a goose, a sharp pecking woman
A woman like a pig, a sleepy-headed woman
A woman like a sickle, a strong stubborn woman
A woman like a goat, a woman of rushing visits
A woman like a sheep, an affable friendly woman
A woman like a lamb, a quiet friendly woman   978

It is not the most beautiful woman
who has the most sense   979

A woman can beat the devil   *   980

A shrew gets her wish but suffers in the getting   981

Work

Many a time the man with ten (cows)
has overtaken the man with forty (cows)   982

Do it as if there was fire in your skin   983

The seeking for one thing will find another   984

Make your hay before the fine weather leaves you   985

Sow early and mow early   986

The early riser gets through his business
but not through early rising   987

The slow horse reaches the mill 988

Making the beginning is one third of the work 989

The quiet pigs eat all the draff 990

The sweat of one's brow is what burns everyone 991

Everyone lays a burden on the willing horse 992

Every little makes a mickle 993

Speed and accuracy do not agree 994

Never put off tomorrow what you can do today 995

I'll go there tonight for evening is speedier
than morning 996

The person of the greatest talk is the person
of the least work 997

Be there with the day and be gone with the day 998

About evening a man is known 999

Long churning makes bad butter 1000

Scattering is easier than gathering 1001

The labour of the crow 1002

Put it on your shoulder and say it is not a burden 1003

It's no delay to stop to edge the tool 1004

The mason who strikes often is better
than the one who strikes too hard 1005

It destroys the craft not to learn it 1006

The dog that's always on the go, is better than
the one that's always curled up 1007

Handfuls make a load 1008

Don't go early or late to the well 1009

A good beginning is half the work 1010

Youth Praise the young and they will make progress 1011

Many a shabby colt makes a fine horse 1012

The young shed many skins 1013

Youth likes to wander 1014

The growth of the gosling 1015

Youth cannot believe 1016

The Triads

TRIADS

Three *as good as*	Three things as good as the best: dirty water to quench a fire, a frieze coat on a frosty day and black bread in famine time. **1017**

Three things that are as good as things better
than them: a wooden sword in a coward's hand,
an ugly wife married to a blind man and
poor clothes on a drunken man.   **1018**

Three best   Three best friends and three worst enemies:
fire, wind and rain.   **1019**

Three best to have in plenty:
sunshine, wisdom, and generosity.   **1020**

Three best things to have a surplus of:
money after paying the rent, seed after spring
and friends at home.   **1021**

Three best invitations: come to mass,
come and make secure and come to the mill.   **1022**

Three with best sight: the eye of a blacksmith
on a nail, the eye of a young girl at a contest
and the eye of a priest on his parish.   **1023**

Three best small:
a beehive, a sheep, and a woman.   **1024**

The three best sounds: the sound of the flail,
the sound of the quern, the sound of the churn.   **1024a**

Three fortunes   The three fortunes of the cat:
the housewife's forgetfulness,
walking without a sound,
and keen sight in darkness.   1025

Three fortunes of the lucky man:
fences, vigilance, and early rising.   1026

Three fortunes of the unlucky man:
long visits to his neighbours, long morning sleep
and bad fences.   1027

Three hardest   The three hardest to go through:
a waterfall, a bog and a briary track.   1028

The three hardest to select:
a Sunday woman, an autumn sheep
and an old mare's foal. 1029

Three kinds

The three kinds of brain:
brain as hard as stone,
brain as receptive as wax and
brain as unstable as flowing water. 1030

The three kinds of men:
the worker, the pleasure-seeker and the boaster. 1031

The three kinds of men who fail
to understand women:
young men, old men and
middle-aged men. 1032

The three kinds of men who rise earliest:
the husband of a talkative wife,
the man with a stolen white horse,
and the man withthe dirty tattered shirt. 1033

The three kinds of poor people:
the man poor by the will of God,
the man poor by his own will and
the man poor even if he owned the world. 1034

The three kinds of women: the woman as
shameless as a pig: the woman as unruly as a hen
and the woman as gentle as a lamb. 1035

Three most

The three most bothersome things in the world:
a thorn in the foot, a woman and a goat going
to the fair that will go anyway but
the way you want it. 1036

The three most delightful things to see:
a garden of white potatoes covered in blossom,
a ship under sail and a woman after giving birth.   1037

The three most difficult to select:
a woman, a scythe and a razor.   1038

The three most difficult to teach:
a mule, a pig and a woman.   1039

The three most difficult to understand:
the mind of a woman, the labour of the bees
and the ebb and flow of the tide.   1040

The three most fortunate things a man ever had:
a mare, a sow and a goose.   1041

The three most nourishing foods: beef marrow,
the flesh of a chicken, Scandinavian beer.   1042

The three most pleasant things:
a cat's kitten, a goat's kid and
a young widow-woman.   1043

The three most troubled eyes:
the eye of a blacksmith after the nail,
the eye of a chicken after the grain and
the eye of a girl seeking her sweetheart.   1043a

Three traits	Three traits of a bull: a bold walk, a strong neck and a hard forehead.	1044
	Three traits of a fox: a light step, a look to the front and a glance to each side of the road.	1045
	Three traits of a hare: a lively ear, a bright eye and a quick run against the hill.	1046
	Three traits of a woman: a broad bosom, a slender waist and a short back.	1047
Three ugliest	The three ugliest things that are: a hairless mangy dog, a woman without flesh or blood, and a deceitful, shameless girl.	1048
	The three ugliest things of their own kind: a thin red-haired woman, a thin yellow horse and a thin white cow.	1049
Three useless	The three things useless when old: an old schoolmaster, an old horse and an old soldier.	1050
	Three things that are of little use: a trumpet and no tongue, a button and no buttonhole and a wolf without teeth.	1051
Three worst	The three worst departures: leaving mass before it ends, leaving table without grace and leaving your wife to go to another woman.	1052

The three worst endings:
the last days of a noble old lady,
the last days of an old white horse
and the last days of an old schoolmaster   1053

The three worst endings: a house burning;
a ship sinking and an old white horse dying.   1053a

The three worst pets:
a pet priest, a pet beggar and a pet pig.   1054

The three worst things to have in a house:
a scolding wife, a smokey chimney and a leaky roof. 1055

The three worse things of all: small, soft potatoes,
from that to an uncomfortable bed and
to sleep with a bad woman.   1056

Three things   The things that cannot be acquired:
voice, generosity and poetry.   1057

Three things that arrive unnoticed:
rent, age and a beard.   1058

Three things to beware of: the hoof of the horse,
the horn of the bull and the smile of the Saxon.   1059

Three things a man should not boast of:
the size of his purse, the beauty of his wife
and the sweetness of his beer.   1060

Three things bright at first, then dull and
finally black: co-operation, a marriage alliance
and living in the one house.   1061

Three things Christ never intended: a woman
whistling, a hound howling and a hen crowing.   1062

Three Things

Three things that relate to drink:
to pay for it, to drink it and to carry it. 1063

Three things that fill a haggard:
ambition, industry and constant vigilance. 1064

Three good things to have: a clean shirt,
a clean conscience and a guinea in the pocket. 1065

Three disagreeable things at home:
a scolding wife, a squalling child
and a smoky chimney. 1066

Three things that don't bear nursing:
an old woman, a hen and a sheep. 1067

Three things that are purposeless:
throwing a stone on a bend,
giving advice to a wrathful woman,
talking to a head without sense. 1068

Three things that remain longest in a family:
fighting, red-hair and thieving. 1069

Three things that don't remain: a white cow,
a handsome woman and a house on a height. 1070

Three things that can never return: a Sunday
without mass, a day away from school and
a day away from work. 1071

Three things that won't have rest: a steep
waterfall, an otter and a devil out of hell. 1072

Three things that never rust:
a woman's tongue,
the shoes of a butcher's horse and
charitable people's money. 1073

Three Things

Three things that never rust:
a sword, a spade and a thought.   1074

Three things never seen:
a blade's edge, wind and love.   1075

Three sharpest things that are: a hound's tooth,
a thorn in the mud and a fool's word.   1076

The three sharpest things:
a fool's word, a thorn in the mud
and a soft woollen thread that cuts to the bone.   1077

Three things that survive for the shortest time:
a woman's association, the love of a mare
for her foal and fresh oaten bread.   1078

Three thing swiftest in the sea:
the seal, the ray and the mackerel.   1079

Three things swiftest on land:
the hound, the hare and the fox.   1080

Three things that leave the shortest traces:
a bird on a branch, a ship on the sea
and a man on a woman.   1081

Three things that leave the longest traces:
charcoal on wood, a chisel on a block of stone
and a ploughshare on a furrow.   1082

Three things not to be trusted:
a fine day in winter, the life of an old person
or the word of an important man unless it's in
writing.   1083

Three things not be trusted:
a cow's horn, a dog's tooth and a horse's hoof.   1084

Three things of least value in any house:
too many geese in a house without a lake,
too many women in a house without wool
to be spun, too many horses in a house
without ploughing to be done.   1085

Three things that have little value:
the head of a woodcock, the head of a goat
and the head of a gurnet.   1086

Three things a man should not be without:
a cat, a chimney and a housewife.   1087

Miscellaneous Three parts of the body most easily hurt:
the knee, the elbow and the eye.   1088

Three that do not clean their snouts:
the farmer, the dog and the pig.   1089

Three coldest things that are:
a hound's snout, a man's knee
and a woman's breast.   1090

Three to whom it's little sense to pay a compliment:
an old man, a bad man and a child.   1091

Miscellaneous

Three deaths that ought not be bemoaned:
the death of a fat hog, the death of a thief
and the death of a proud prince.   1092

Three the devil has without much trouble:
the mason, the bailiff and the miller.   1093

Three enemies of the body: wind, smoke and fleas.   1094

Three errors relating to corn: to cut it green,
to grind it damp and to eat it fresh.   1095

Three great evils: smallness of house,
closeness of heart and shortage of food.   1096

Three with the sharpest eyes:
a hawk on a tree, a fox in a glen,
a young girl at a meeting.   1097

Three wholesome foods for the driver:
the back of a herring, the belly of a salmon
and the head of a thrush (moorhen).   1098

Three bad habits:
drinking the glass, smoking the pipe
and scattering the dew late at night.   1099

Three happiest in the world:
the tailor, the piper and the goat.   1100

Three strokes that are keeping Ireland:
the stroke of an axe on a block,
of a hammer on an anvil
and of a threshing flail in the centre.   1101

Three jobs that must be done with vigour:
rowing, hammering and measuring the ground
with your fist *(ie. using the sickle)*.   1102

Miscellaneous

Three kind acts unrequited:
that done for an old man, for a wicked person
or for a little child. 1103

Three sweetest melodies: the churning of butter,
the plough ploughing and the mill grinding. 1104

Three oaths that money swore:
that it did not care who would possess it,
that it would stay but a while with any man
and that it would not stay with any man but the
man who loved it. 1105

Three pair that never agree:
two married women in the same house,
two cats with one mouse
and two bachelors after the one young woman. 1106

Three places that cannot be avoided:
the place of birth, the place of death
and the place of burial. 1107

Three times it is most likely to rain:
early on Friday, late on Saturday and
on Sunday morning when it's time for first mass. 1108

Three greatest rushes: the rush of water,
the rush of fire and the rush of falsehood. 1109

Three sauciest by nature: a ram, a bull and a tailor. 1110

Three skills of the hare: sharp turning,
high jumping, and strong running against the hill. 1111

Three strongest forces: the force of fire,
the force of water and the force of hatred. 1112

Three truths: sunrise, sunset and death. 1113

Miscellaneous — Three unluckiest things to meet first thing in the morning: a mad dog, a man who lent you money and a red-haired girl.   1114

Three virtues of the drunkard: a miserable morning, a dirty coat and an empty pocket.   1115

Three signs of an unfortunate man: going bail, intervening in disputes and giving evidence.   1115a

The three characteristics of the Fianna: purity of heart: strength of limb, and acting according to our word.   1115b

Four ... — Four priests who are not greedy: four Frenchmen who are not yellow (cowardly); four cobblers who don't tell lies; that's twelve not in this country.   1116

Four things an Irishman should not trust: a cow's horn, a horse's hoof, a dog's snarl and an Englishman's laugh. *(Compare 1059)*   1117

The four fortunes of the cat: the housewife's error: walking without care; no water in milk, and sight at night as well as by day. *(Compare 1025)*   1118

Four hateful things: a worthless hound, a slow horse, a chief without wisdom and a wife without children.   1119

NOTES

Proverbs 50 & 707	The buailtin is part of the flail that strikes the corn.
Proverb 51	Ciotog is the Irish word for a left-handed person; it often implies awkwardness. In this instance, however, the implication is one of the cuteness or guile. Various superstitions are associated with the ciotog – including suspicion of evil or treachery (note the English word 'sinister', from the latin).
Proverb 55	The Irish word 'meitheal' means a team of workers (neighbours) assisting one another at turf-cutting or hay-making. The blacksmith usually had the largest meitheal in the parish since his work at the forge was of such importance to the community.
Proverb 60	'The Old Woman of Beare' – a legendary figure in Irish folklore and poetry. (See Padraic Pearse's poem, *Mise Eire*, and Austin Clarke's, *The Young Woman of Beare*).
Proverb 71	About 300 a.d. when Corman MacArt was High King of Ireland, ruling from Tara, a warrior army called the Fianna was formed under the leadership of Fionn MacCumhaill. Around the Fianna and its leader grew a great body of legend still popular today. Fionn himself was noted for his bravery and wisdom (he tasted the salmon of knowledge). The Fianna eventually became too powerful for the High King but were defeated at the battle of Gabhra and disbanded.

Proverb 203a   The word 'cess', according to P.W. Joyce, may mean a contraction of success, or a 'contribution'. He refers to its use in County Louth as meaning a quantity of corn in for threshing.

Proverb 271   Lough Sheelin is a large lake in County Cavan

Proverb 441   Used as a reply when you are reminded by someone of a favour he has granted you.

Proverb 595 & 598   'Speckled' refers to the 'heat-spots' got on the shins from sitting too long and too close by the fire.

Proverb 716   This proverb is King Diarmuid's famous judgement, given about 560 a.d., on the ownership of a manuscript copy made by St Colmcille of a manuscript belonging to St Finnian. It must be one of our first copyright laws.

Index of Key Words

Ability 1-7, 668

Absence 390, 635

Accuracy 994

Achievement 254

Acknowledge 150

Acquire (to) 1057

Act 299, 1103, 1115b

Action 880

Address (to) 420

Advice 8-13, 656, 1068

Affectation 14-17

Affection 626

Afraid 338, 339

Afternoon 638

Age 18-26, 668, 843, 1058

Agree (to) 994, 1106

Ale 467

Alehouse 881

Alive 874

Alliance 1061

Allot 458

Alms 148, 156

Alone 411

Amadan 365, 367

Ambition 1064

Angel 17

Anger 27-30, 443, 899

Answer 443

Anvil 1101

Apart 583

Appear 181

Appearance 31-37

Apple 695, 719

Apple-tree 695

Apply (to) 592

April 820, 934

Apron 974

Arm 166

Army 552

Arrive (to) 1058

Art 38

As...as 39-77b

Ashes 25, 29

Ass 199

Attack (to) 552

Author 787, 814

Authority 862

Autumn 598, 821, 1029

Avoid (to) 1107

Axe 1101

Bachelors 1106

Back 225, 253, 256, 521, 1047

Backside 596

Bad 43, 91, 101, 145, 168, 203-203a, 302, 305-306, 682, 815, 876, 908, 916, 953, 1000, 1056, 1099

Bag 426

Bagpipes 675

Bail 1115a

Bailiff 1093

Bald 50

Ball 555

Baptise (to) 161

Barb 237

Bard 30

Bare 168, 596

Barefoot 970

Bargain 884

Bark 347

Bark (to) 3, 420, 584, 935, 962

Barrington 43

Bashful 68

Beak 294

Beard 1058

Beast 932

Beat (to) 292, 836